West End
as I remember it
Edited by Karen Barrow

Leicestershire
Libraries & Information Service

Editor and some of the prize-winners of the West End as I remember it competition. Left to right – Karen Barrow (Editor); Mr. Clarke (4th); Mrs. Taylor (2nd); Mr. Williams (1st); Mr. Creasey (3rd); Mr. Ashby (5th). (Photograph courtesy of the Leicester Mercury.)

INTRODUCTION

The West End was the second venue for Leicestershire Libraries' series of "As I remember it" competitions. Like the first competition, held in Belgrave, it was not only a very rewarding local history project but also a very successful creative writing project as people were invited to send in their written or taped memories of the area before 1950.

The West End is perhaps not as clearly defined as Belgrave, and so the first problem was to decide just what *was* the West End. For the purposes of the competition, it was eventually decided to include Woodgate, Newfoundpool, Westcotes and Rowley Fields, roughly following the boundaries of Wyngate Drive and the old railway line.

Much time and effort was spent in publicising the competition – not only by distributing posters and leaflets but also by visiting Evergreen Clubs, Homes and Drop Ins in the area; and by appearances on Centre Radio and Radio Leicester. At this point our thanks must go to Age Concern, who helped with the distribution of our publicity and donated one of our prizes. Our special thanks go to Radio Leicester as the two phone in programmes on "Crosstalk" resulted in a flood of enquiries and entries from near and far – even from as far away as Nottingham and Grantham. It was particularly interesting to note that a good proportion of entries submitted were from people who no longer live in the West End; and that because of the varying ages of the entrants, tended to cover different periods of time.

We received about ninety entries, fourteen of which were submitted on tape. Some people asked specifically *not* to be considered for the competition, because they had found that writing there memories down had been a rewarding enough experience on its own. The panel of judges had quite an arduous task before them! The standard of entries was in fact so high that an additional five consolation prizes were awarded, making 10 prizewinners altogether. The prizegiving took place in September 1983 at Westcotes Library, hosted by Morgan Cross of Radio Leicester, who had also arranged for the event to be broadcast live.

This booklet contains extracts from the 10 prizewinning entries. They neither were nor are intended as a social documentary or criticism, but are, quite simply, very enjoyable and readable memories of homes, shops, schools and social life in the West End. Finally, a phrase which appeared time and again throughout the competition neatly summarises the enduring affection all our entrants have for the area – the following quote comes from Mr. Clarke's entry:-

'One still sees familiar faces and if you were to ask them they would say, what we used to say all those years ago – West End . . . Best End.'

Mr. F.H. Williams now of Faire Road, Glenfield, writes of "the Pool" before 1936. His grandparents lived on the Pool from 1890 and Mr. Williams, himself, has been a 'West Ender' all his life.

The 'Pool' comprises that area of the West End of Leicester off the Fosse Road North which includes Beatrice Road, Pool Road and the nine streets which span between these two. It is interesting to note that the initial letters of all the street names form the name of the builder and developer – I. (Isaac) Harrison and also, that Beatrice Road was named after his daughter.

Basically the 'Pool' was a village community even though it was part of the city. To the south it was bounded by allotments, to the west were fields through to Glenfields and to the north were more allotments and fields as far as the eye could see. It was an island stuck on the West End of Leicester and this fact is of considerable significance when considering the characters of the inhabitants. The development of the area commenced around the latter part of the 19th Century when the Great Central Railway was forging its line through to the north, in addition to building the railroad the company also built a number of houses and the 'Pool' has more than its fair share of them. The area owes a lot to the Great Central since a large number of railway workers were housed in these exceedingly good houses. It did not stop there as the comradeship of the railway workers, their love of their job, their loyalty to both the 'Company' and each other, spilled over into the community. One recalls with nostalgia the conversations held in the early hours of the morning between the 'Knocker Up' and his victim and the selfless way to which it was responded.

The character of the 'Pool' can to some extent be seen through the shops which catered for the total requirements of the community. The businesses were all family concerns not a single multiple or national store (that is if one ignores the 'Co-op' on Fosse Road). The Post Office, as it is today, was the centre of activity, kept by the Watson sisters (not forgetting their Airedale dogs). They knew most people by name including the children. They were privy to much personal information of the inhabitants, looking after the only savings they had, receiving the telegrams giving the joys and grief of the people – if they had not respected their unique position what a wealth of stories they could have told. No family would exist without meat and the 'Pool' was well served by four butchers.

One must recall with pleasure the Pork Butcher's shop of Mr. Sibson (5 foot nothing and large moustache) and remember those delicious hot faggots and mushy peas for which he was so renowned. He also sold home rendered lard, out of large tins, which was spread on slices of bread baked by Tebbutts Bakery on Pool Road. This formed a staple food for a number of inhabitants. The bakery on Pool Road allowed the use of its ovens on Christmas Day to cook the Christmas dinners. Another delicacy of the day was catered for by Eames Tripe Shop. Every Friday night there were queues of people with jugs eager to buy the tripe of their choice – Reed, Seam or Honeycomb – piping hot and immersed in delicious liqueur. On Sunday morning at the crack of dawn the Eames sold hot Cow-heels straight from the copper and skinned while you waited. As a by-product of this business Neatsfoot oil was produced and sold for numerous medicinal purposes. The grocers shops bring back wonderful memories. The two main provision merchants were King's and Chapmans both were very much alike with Kings being the larger. As soon as you entered the shop you were confronted by a lovely aroma and there in front of you were rows upon rows of biscuit tins, all with glass tops displaying all kinds and brands of biscuits. The sides of bacon hung from the metal hooks in the ceiling awaiting your order – Plain, Smoked, Home Cured, Cumberland Cured, etc. As a child, all you probably wanted was ½d worth of broken biscuits and what a feast we had!

Smaller grocers shops did exist and one must mention Mrs Hart and her gentle ways and understanding of peoples' problems. Operating from her small shop converted from a 'Railway House' she would supply groceries on 'Tick' and would always include a free bag of sweets with the weekly groceries.

Furniture, both new and secondhand could be bought at Marshall's and Neal's and of course at Case's the Pawnbrokers. Prior to the 1939-45 war the pawnbroker played a very important part in the life of the community and nowhere was this better evidenced than on the 'Pool'. Loans would be raised on whatever could be 'hocked', probably some family heirlooms of great sentimental value, to be redeemed when the money was available – often out of Friday night's pay in order that the article could be used for the weekend – only to go back into 'hock' on the following Monday morning.

There were two dairies on the 'Pool' – Gilfords on Pool Road and Hawley's at the corner of Beatrice Road and Ruby Street. The milk and eggs were brought in fresh every morning and straight from local farms. You were served direct from the 'churn', the amount measured with the special ½ pint or 1 pint utensil. The home made ice cream made by Hawley's was delicious and came in ½d cornets, 1d cornets and 2d wafer in either raspberry flavour or vanilla.

No report on the shops of the 'Pool' would be complete without a special mention for the General Store (also in a converted Railway House), run by Mrs. Smith. She sold needles, yarns, sweets, toys, aprons, canes (for punishing wayward children), fly papers and dozens of other things. But the things she will be most remembered for are the delicious home made lemonade and herb beer and in season the toffee apples – the apples were of course from their own allotment. How did she produce ice cream without a freezer or refrigerator?

Play for the children of the 'Pool' held few problems – the days were never long enough to do all the things you wished to do. Ball games could be played in the streets with complete safety even on the main Beatrice Road.

More dangerous games included 'Last across the Road', played I hasten to add with horse and dray, or even to hanging onto the back of them. Remember the old cry warning the drayman, 'Whip, Whip Behind!'? At this you would immediately drop off and run for cover. For the more daring and with the advent of buses round the 'Pool' you could hang on to the rear lower door hinge, put your feet on the spare wheel and get a lift from Hawthorne Street to Fosse Road. The bus was affectionately known as 'Red Emma'. A day off school or during holidays the children would take packed lunches and wander off to the canal at Northgates for a day's fishing and mischief or venture across the fields to Glenfields. This latter was a favourite venue since there were so many ways of getting there. By going via Hospital Lane onto the London Midland & Scottish Swannington Railway Line one could get an

Fosse Road in the 19th century. (Illustration by Paul Barrand from an original photograph courtesy of the Leicester Mercury.)

arrow head made by placing a 6" nail on the track and let the good old 1890 Loco flatten it for you – very useful when later in the day you hopefully arrived at that paradise in Glenfields known as the '52 Steps', near the celebrated Tunnel. (Are there any lads who never ventured through the Tunnel?)

No essay on the 'Pool' would be complete without a mention of some of the characters. There was the local vicar 'Beaky Edmunds' who put the fear of god into people in a way which was not intended by his calling. In order to admonish his parishioners for non-attendance at church he would summon them to the front door by banging his umbrella on the fanlight. Children were petrified of him! Then there was Mr. Hughes the six foot School Board man riding his twin cross bar cycle around the area – heaven help you if you were playing truant!

Then in 1936 came urban sprawl and slum clearance – the insular position of the 'Pool' was drawing to a close. Gradually it was surrounded by what is now New Parks Estate but what will always be known to the inhabitants of the Newfoundpool as 'Freaks Estate'. I am conscious that this is a mis-spelling but I feel it sums up the resentment felt by a number of people at the passing of an era. Luckily, visitors to the area can still find the same great community spirit. Long may it survive.

Mrs. Taylor has also spent the major part of her life in the Newfoundpool area. She came to Leicester in 1915, lived first on Upperton Road, moving to Pool Road when she married, where she lived for 53 years! Her essay which concentrates on the Westcotes area, was written on paper taken from a book she has kept since the twenties, in which she writes verses and quotations.

I started to attend Narborough Road Infant School after Christmas – January 1916 – then went to Robert Hall Chapel rooms – an "overflow" from the main school, then back to Narborough Road Senior part. It was said that this school was the best elementary school in Leicester – very up to date. It boasted a cookery school, and girls from other schools around came for a day's training each week for a year, from the top class. There were cookery and laundry rooms and a well furnished dining room cum parlour, bedroom and a bathroom – where we learnt to bath the baby, though in those days at twelve or thirteen, many of us were ignorant about how babies were "begotten"!

In those days of class distinction I suppose we lived in an upper working class area. Our house had four bedrooms including an attic and two toilets. Even in the West End, "the Best End", as some called it, there were many families living in streets off Hinckley and King Richards Road, who had to share with others. A number of children around us went to private schools – there were several 'Kindergartens' run by spinster ladies, the most popular being Miss Andrew's, now Fosse High School.

I have always regretted missing out on a better education which practically finished at thirteen, as I was in the top class for two years. However at fourteen, I obtained work in the office of the Magic Polish Company, Western Road, at the princely wage of 10/- per week – 8.30 a.m. to 6 p.m. and 8.30 to 12 on Saturdays. This was a 'family firm' established, I think, in 1891 by Mr. Dick Potter. He was Manager of the Equity Co-op Boot and Shoe Company on Western Road prior to establishing the Magic and I understand he had a big hand in building Equity Road. It was a thriving business in those days.

Going up Hinckley Road there were shops and houses to Fosse Road. There was a chapel on the left corner, now belonging to the Ukrainians. Fosse Road was built up. There was an orphanage further on towards King Richards Road, later turned into houses, now gone in the West Bridge Scheme. At the corner of Kirby Road was a private school, Kelland College, now St. Paul's Church Rooms. At the corner of the Fosse and Glenfield Road was a large house. During the first war a party of nuns escaped from war-torn France and started a school-Convent of the Nativity.

Our family attended St. Peter's Church, Leamington Street. The Parish Priest for very many years was Father Caus, later Canon, a Belgian. He was a tall handsome man striding around visiting parishioners, a well known figure. I remember another well known character, the Rev. Rosalie Lee, Minister at the Unitarian Chapel on Narborough Road, near Westcotes Drive. She was much loved, especially by the young girls. I think she was the first lady Minister in Leicester, probably in the country. She was a very imposing figure in her black robes. I can remember going to some gathering with a friend who attended the Church and felt very uncomfortable when she said to me 'you are not one of my flock are you?'

We lived next door to Eyres (Painters and Decorators) – in fact they owned our house. Their office and stores were across the road. A few houses from us lived Coulsons (Builders) – their yard was beside their house. Further towards Narborough Road was the Lacey Family – he was a Blacksmith and often had a crowd of kids watching him. I felt worried in case the horses were being hurt. Later on, when the motor car and lorry were replacing horse traffic, they turned the business into a garage – father and son.

Our newsagents were Mills at the corner of Wilberforce Road and Upperton Road – the bridge side.

They were also barbers and I think I was about their first female customer when I had my hair 'bobbed'. Later they started a ladies hairdressing business.

On the other side of Upperton Road past Wilberforce Road was Tarratt's off-licence, and a fish and chip shop which I frequented often – their name was Food! On the opposite side of Narborough Road was a hardware shop from where I fetched gas mantles, and the Co-op. My cousin used to send me there on a Friday evening to buy cream cakes – gorgeous cream oozing out – 2d each. There was a Chinese laundry where every week I took Uncle's collars and fetched the other lot back. He had a clean one every day – I think they charged 1d each and oh! the heat – I felt sorry for them. You could see them slaving away in the room behind – a woman and two men.

There was a garage – Needham's – my uncle bought a Rover Eight in 1924 and kept it there. My Aunt was annoyed about this purchase for it cost about £180. She said he was too old to learn to drive and was nervous unless he had a relative with them who was an experienced driver. No driving tests then – he bought the car from Sturgesses (Braunstone Gate) – was taken out for several lessons and that was it. I loved going 'runs' with him on Sunday mornings with one or other of my friends. Cars were becoming quite common then – still plenty of horses about but gradually being taken over by motor driven vans and lorries.

Boys would gather to play 'pitch and toss' and various marble and 'fag' card games. Some played for money-farthings and halfpennies, but were careful to watch for the 'bobby'. Another popular game was the wooden hoop. Boys were very adept at running with these large hoops, guiding them with a stick.

I feel I must mention trips to Glenfield from West Bridge Station. These were put on during holidays. Hundreds of children packed the small platform. We were bundled in the carriages and carefully locked in. Most of the short journeys went under the tunnel – we weren't allowed out until we were safely back. I think the cost was 2d.

Memories still come flooding in – the General Election, for instance. I remember seeing Winston Churchill going into Narborough Road School. He wore a large black hat and an astrakhan collar. I think he stood as a Conservative – the West End was usually Liberal. Anyway, he lost. I also remember Ramsey MacDonald standing for Labour – he also lost – he lived on Wolverton Road or around there for sometime.

Mr. Creasey's entry was one of many submitted on tape. Mr Creasey was born in Braunstone Gate and now lives in Norman Street.

I remember standing in the front room watching the men laying the tram track along Braunstone Gate. Starting with shops there was a butcher's shop inside New Parks Street named Cuffling whose window display had a half circle cut out so that he could reach and get his meat from the window, because he was very bonny. Then there was Casey's Pawn Shop on the corner. We used to stand there as children and watch the London to Nottingham Express train at 5 o'clock in the evening and see the last coach leaving the rest of the train. Then there was Tuckwood's Cake Shop and next door to there was Burton's. They made their own ice-cream which was out-of-this-world. At the corner of Thorpe Street there was a coffee house owned by Mr. Bennett. There was another coffee house on West Bridge and yet another at the corner of Great Holme Street and Hinckley Road. And a Mr. Woods had a sadler's shop making harnesses; Bloxham's the Fish Shop; a tailor's owned by Mr. Carrington and an umbrella shop owned by Mr. Hearn.

The first school I went to was St. Mary's in Castle St. When Narborough School was opened I went there and I still remember playing in the sand-pit. After that I went to Shaftesbury Street. I was there when King George V was crowned King of England. That was on June the 22nd, 1911 and we all had a tin of chocolate and a medal. As regards games and social life we used to go to the Boulevard Pictures on Saturday afternoons for 1d or roller-skating at the rink next door, or spend an hour or so on the swings next to the rink. At the corner of Bede Street and the Gate was wasteland and every Bank Holiday Johnny Monk would bring his fair with the galloping horses and sideshows with the oil players. The first time I saw it, he would take a section of the platform out and put a pony inside and off it would go. But some time later he turned up with a traction engine and made his own power and lighting. What a lovely sight in those days it was!

The corner of Bridge Street and Castle Street in the late 19th century. (Illustration by Paul Barrand from an original photograph courtesy of the Leicester Mercury.)

Now up the Narborough Road. I'm getting a bit older now, and I remember Bismarck Street, which has been changed to Beaconsfield Road and the Olympia Picture House. I remember that being built in 1912. The bricklayers used to work nightshifts, light obtained from the overhead tram cables.

Then at the corner of Imperial Avenue and the Narborough Road were two fields owned by cattle dealers, Hull and Flannigan. Flannigan's half is still there. From there you went up by the allotment to the hunting field. They used to bring the horses from Freeschool Lane to exercise them there. The Braunstone Hotel stands there now and the Roxy Pictures and beyond that you're in the country. At the corner of Fosse Road and Upperton Road the Braunstone Park fields would start, only you had to cross the Burton Railway Line on the journey. I remember the park on Winchester Avenue being opened. It was called for a long time the Penny Park. Every child who was at the opening received a new penny.

For personalities there was Miss Biddle who kept the Tripe House in Red Cross Street and for 6d you could have your chimney swept by Kelly, a seventeen stone man who lived in Great Holme Street and on Sunday afternoon Mr. Riddington would come round with his basket shouting 'shrimps and winkles'. Then there was Ducky Sims who toured Ridley Street. He was shouting 'Penny a pint, milk', and that little fellow who used to walk about the town with a sandwich board and a silk top hat, and used to live on Foxon Street. The more popular gentlemen were Mr. Wand who had chemist shops around the town, one of which was on Narborough Road; a Mr. Crow who owned a furnishing shop at the corner of Bond Street and Eastgate; Mr Charlesworth who owned a dyeworks which were used by Kirby and West for their bottling plant and Mr. W.A. Spencer, the Estate Agent. All these people were members of St. Mary's Church.

I remember seeing two bullocks pulling a cart down Narborough Road displaying a brand of suet and seeing the Quorn hounds and huntsmen coming down Narborough Road after a day's hunting. I walked with them to the Great Central Station where they were put in vans to take them back to the kennels. I remember seeing the Desford Reformatory School Boys' Band all dressed in corduroy suits and pill-box hats playing in the streets. And what about the old lamplighter with his flame on a pole? I remember the Boulevard coal wharf where you had to scramble for a truck to push your coal home at the price of 4d, 5d, 6d per hundredweight. The same applied to Westbridge wharf not far from the Westbridge Railway Station and King Dick's Road School. The barge on the the canal named 'Heart of Oak' was filled with coal. Three men would barrow it on until it was full then a horse would pull it to St. Mary's Rubber Mills and the same three men would barrow it to the boiler house. I remember the carrier's cart coming down Narborough Road and Hinckley Road with their wares and parking at the Blue Boar pub next to Everard's Brewery in Southgate.

Castle Gardens are a lovely place now but when I was a boy it was in two parts – the Newarke Street end was worked by a market gardener and the Castle Street end was a corporation yard to cut out the kerb stones, granite pits, gravel and sand for all the area. I remember the town waites coming round in the early morning playing carols at Christmas time and they would finish with 'Good morning, Mr. and Mrs. So-and-So' at past two o'clock. Where I live now were two engine drivers on the Central Railway and the knocker-up would come at one o'clock in the morning and wake them up and shout 'Sheds at one' or one of these times. He used to wake the whole neighbourhood. The West End was the Best End.

Mr. Clarke, of Bembridge Road, was born in Celt Street and says he was brought up to pronounce it KELT Street. In 1930 his mother ran a small general store at 81 Cranmer street. Mr. Clarke was Leicestershire's Sabre Champion in 1958.

It is known as the Junction and it is where Narborough road, Hinckley road and Braunstone Gate meet. At the hub was a gentlemens' lavatory and a stone drinking trough (said by some to be Richard III's coffin). These were much appreciated by man and beast respectively. In this area of the West End lived a community almost self supporting in every way. There was a very cheap and reliable tram service to all parts of the city. The library was the most distinctive building around here and inside it was dark, panelled and silent. We tiptoed in without a whisper to change our books.

Every type of shop was close by, usually managed by an obliging owner. Some names that will bring back memories are:- On Narborough road at the Junction was Monks – furniture removals; Brooks – general store; Bowers – tailors; Leedhams – for cycles etc. It was here we took our accumulators to be re-charged to power our valve wireless sets. On the other side of the road was Mr. American, later Mr. Mendham, and later still Mr. Clow, all dentists. Next door lived a musical family named Groocock. One of the three daughters taught classical dancing.

Further up the road was a Chinese laundry. Hinckley road saw Mr. North serving meat; Hensons for fish and chips; Mrs. Smith for millinery; Mr. Lenton for shoe repairs; and Mr. Vickers started his flourishing flower shop. On the opposite side Willie Bush and his Mum ran the finest music shop in town and next door was the Post Office. In Braunstone Gate was Mr. Allen's hairdressing salon with Youngs the pork butchers close by. Mr. Gadsby opened his first Art Shop here. Bloxhams did a good trade in wet fish and poultry and on Bede street corner Albert White had his newsagents shop. At the bottom of Westcotes Drive there was Dr. Cooper and Dr. Greer and opposite was Wands the chemists. At the corner of Roman street was Squires Bakery. Silent black and white films were shown for our enjoyment at the 'Olympia' (Narborough road) 'Tudor' (Vaughan street), later at the 'Westleigh' on Fosse road.

The games we played were varied and provided healthy exercise. Girls enjoyed skipping and boys loved 'Weak 'Osses'. Snobs were popular and were made by sewing shoe buttons together. Other games were hop scotch, leap frog and whip and top. Hoops kept our legs moving and marbles were always exciting. The 'choc' for this game was made by removing the soil from between the cobblestones in the street. Skimming and collecting cigarette cards was big business, particularly the silken ones of various flags.

The front room of every house in our street opened onto the pavement. Houses with even numbers had three upstairs rooms and three downstairs. Those with odd numbers had two upstairs and three downstairs. Every two houses shared a yard plus a bit of garden with one outside toilet between them. In the kitchen was a coal fired copper with copper stick for stirring the clothes. After boiling the clothes they were plunged and agitated in a dolly tub. Wooden dolly pegs were used for this purpose. The wet wash was then put through a mangle which consisted of an iron frame with two wooden rollers. These were turned by a spoked cast iron wheel. The washing was then hung to dry or air in the yard if fine or in the entry and indoors if wet. Finally the wash was ironed with a solid flat iron heated by the coal fire.

Coal was fetched in small solid wheel barrows, which held one hundredweight, from the coal wharf on West Bridge. Water was provided by a pump in the yard which was later replaced by a standpipe. The middle room had a cast iron range in three sections. A coal fire filled the centre grate and water was heated in the right hand boiler. On the left was an oven for cooking purposes. The whole range was polished with black lead until it shone and was so useful that a fire was burning most of the year. These houses were lit by gaslight using incandescent mantles. Payment for gas was by a penny in the slot meter. The big advantage of these houses was they were cosy and warm in the winter and cool in the summer and needed a minimum of curtaining and floorcovering. Neighbours were very close and friendly, particularly when cases of hardship or illness were known. Doors were never locked and one was never afraid to go out after dark. When a person was seriously ill, sand and sawdust were spread on the street to deaden the rattle of cartwheels and horses hooves. And when death occurred a black board was screwed to the front window. Black armbands were customary with a black tie for men.

Most children went to Shaftesbury road School and despite its smallness it was one of the most respected, as, invariably it produced the finest athletes in the county. The most notable being Doris (Doll) College, who later became a first class comédienne. On Empire Day all pupils marched round the playground and saluted the flag. Pride in King and Country, respect for teachers and love for parents was instilled into us and remained with us throughout our lives. In later years children were graded. Some went to Narborough road (Westcotes). An excellent school with matching masters. King Richard's road (K.R.R.) affectionately known as Kelly's Rotten Rabbits and those very fine Grammar Schools Wyggeston, Alderman Newton's and City Boys.

If the summer was hot there was always the baths at Bath Lane, one banjo shaped and the other banana shaped. Another favourite with hardy swimmers was Bede House off the canal on Upperton road. In the winter we used to bake potatoes in the oven and roast chestnuts on the fire. Cooking onions were thrown onto the glowing coals until they were quite black. They were then lifted off and the charred exterior removed revealing a pure white, beautifully cooked interior. Salt was added to taste. Salt was bought from a woman who came round with blocks in a barrow. She would saw off as much as required, this was then crushed by a rolling pin and kept in a salt box. Friday night treat was to take a basin of Youngs in Braunstone Gate for some hot pigs belly, with a piece of hodge, and plenty of jiper. Every night at dusk we never tired of watching the lamplighters march out of their little room at the back of the library. The yard in which this stood has now been taken over by the library extensions. Every night they marched out with a little acetylene flame at the end of a pole to light all the gas street lamps in the West End. The same procedure occurred every morning to put the lamps out.

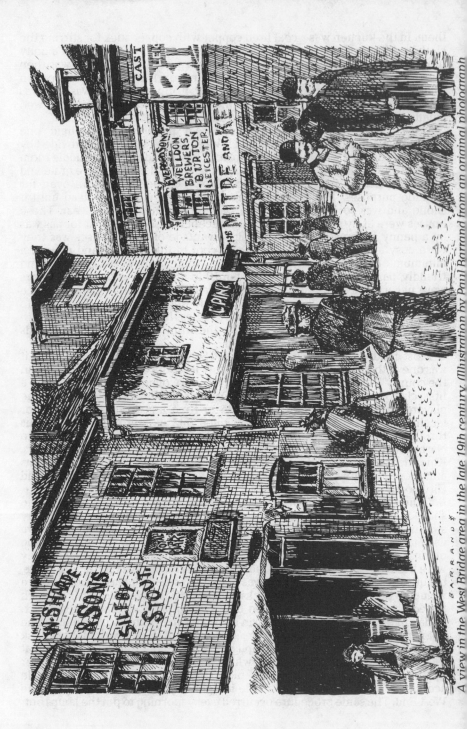

A view in the West Bridge area in the late 19th century. (Illustration by Paul Barratt from an original photograph.)

Mr. Ashby was born in 1898 and has also lived in the West End all his life. He is a keen local historian and in 1981 was invited to assist in preparing the new edition of Pevsner's 'Leicestershire and Rutland'.

In my childhood our journeys into town were by St. Paul's Church and down King Richard's road, which older people still called Watt's Causeway and told us nostalgically of cherry orchards. Shaded by mature trees framing an impressive view of the lofty apse of St. Paul's, the road, though fully built up and the largest shopping centre in the neighbourhood, was very pleasant, and the shops of good quality. They became very familiar. Butler the grocer and Butler the chemist, facing one another at the corners of Clara street, but unrelated to one another: Pickering the butcher and Leesar the pork butcher some distances apart: near the top two confectioners, Coles and Brearley. My mother bought Coles' business in 1905 after my father's death, and we went to live here. At the post office was Brant the stationer and, on the other side lower down, Mason, with whom I usually spent my Saturday penny on one of the W.T. Stead's Books for the Bairns. There were two fishmongers, Swain and Broughton, but my mother bought her fish from Nicholls, of Hinckley road. His daughter came round on her bicycle in the morning for orders and sent it by midday – Smith's the greengrocers was old fashioned with a wet brick floor, open windows and no counter, but children found it friendly. It was kept by an elderly widow and her two daughters. The elder to my perpetual but carefully concealed amusement, was Mrs. Daft. The name of the Newfoundpool Inn seemed in the wrong place. I was at school with Fred Crowhurst who, when he succeeded his father as landlord, altered it to 'The Crow's Nest'.

By 1899 King Richard's road was entered from West Bridge by the new St. Augustine street, under an iron section of the mile long viaduct carrying the main line of the new Great Central Railway, to which the West End owed immense changes in appearance. The road was still served by the horse buses, by modern standards small and slow, but seating about 30 passengers. Straw on the floor on wet or very cold days was the most effective amenity, and conditions could be spartan. But the destination boards on the sides, white lettered on scarlet, gave them a cherry touch, and many drivers and conductors were amusing characters. The service ended with the arrival of the electric trams in 1904. These did not travel along King Richard's road, until in 1915, a new line was constructed there and the Hinckley road section of the Fosse road circular route transferred to it. To provide for this, the Bow Bridge was strengthened and slightly altered in direction. To save wear the rails were interlocked, not fitted with points, and carried cars only in one direction. Even so the track deteriorated and in 1939 the trams reverted to their original route. The track was not repaired as the use of trolley buses was already under consideration. But eventually motor buses were introduced.

About 1930, the railway bridges over Narborough road and the Fosse road south were replaced by heavy ones of iron. These were built on scaffolding alongside the existing bridges, and on successive Sundays the new structure moved on rollers into position, an ingenious operation that those of us who saw it will not forget. But on the Fosse road, the new bridge left insufficient clearance and within a very short time, a tall van became tightly wedged

King Richard's Road, looking towards the city centre. (Illustration by Paul Barrand from an original photograph courtesy of Leicestershire Museums, Art Galleries and Records Service.)

under it, a mishap commemorated to this day by a sharp, twisting dip and rise in the road between high, railed footways.

The focal centre of Fosse road at the beginning of the century seems to have been the five way junction to St. Paul's Church. To the south it was 'the Fosse' simply, without qualification, the best regarded residential centre in the West End, with a number of large detached houses, the homes of successful manufacturers and business men. This position it retained until the Western Park estate was opened up some years later. It had a 'colony' further along on the inner side of the Burton line, and on Westcotes Drive – still called Manor Road by many were – two very gloomy mansions, 'Sykefield', home of the Harris family and 'Westcotes Grange' in dark blue brick. House numbers ran originally from Hinckley road to King Richards road but about this time were reversed to begin at King Richard's road and continue across Hinckley road and along Fosse road south as it extended.

I was well acquainted with one of the large houses, Charnwood House, adjoining the Wesleyan Church, now St. Andrew's, with which it is isolated by the cutting of the new King Richard's road. For until I was four years old it was the home of my grandfather. I still have many memories of family parties, with uncles and aunts coming from as far afield as Scotland and Wales, of playing in the back garden with its splendid view high over the town and of an uncle pretending to climb the monkey puzzle tree in front of the house. Among the houses of the rich was a long, dark building with the inscription 'Infant Orphan Asylum' in porcelain letters across the front. With its long crocodile of girls in grim brownish uniforms it did not of itself add any brightness to the Fosse. But in front of it was a row of magnificently towering poplars 'the Seven Sisters', seen as a landmark not only from Western Park but from right across the town. It was a sad day when they were declared unsafe and felled.

Here on the Fosse were three private schools. One, Kelland College, in the present Church House at the corner of Kirby road, taking boarders. All had relatively long lives, and one, now officially recognised, is still in existence. This is the Fosse High school founded in or about 1898 by Mrs. M. Bond at No. 32. I became a pupil there in March 1903 and in those safer, quieter days I was able to walk to school unaccompanied by way of Danes Hill road. About 1907, after a year with Miss Kelly as headmistress, it was moved to No. 60 and taken over by three sisters, the Misses Neale, in whose hands it remained until long after 1950, though about 1930 they moved it to its present building at the corner of Westcotes Drive. This was built as a school, Froebel House, the third of the schools originating on the central Fosse, and founded by the Misses Andrewes, who were unable to continue. It was a boys' private school, St. George's for about two years before being acquired by the Neales.

After my father's death I had to be withdrawn and sent to a council school. This too was on the Fosse road but near its northern end, a junior school in the buildings of the Primitive Methodist Church. This had been removed piecemeal from the West Bridge to allow the opening of St. Augustine Street, and the stones of the facade were numbered in black, a disfigurement that lingered for years. I was not unhappy there, but the goal set before me was a scholarship to the Wyggeston, which my father and two of his brothers had attended from the opening day in 1877. I gained my scholarship in three years and no longer went to school in the West End. The amateur Leicester Fosse Football Club was founded by a group of Old Wyggestonians living on

Narborough Road, looking South, early 1900's. Note the tram and the houses, all still with their frontages not yet converted to shops. (Illustration by Paul Barrand from an original photograph courtesy of the Leicester Mercury.)

or near Fosse road. My father was a playing member and an uncle the first Secretary.

Mr. Buckley lived at 35 Narborough Road, from childhood until 1949, but remained in close contact with the area until 1966. He has recently retired from a post in the Department of Mathematics at the University of Leicester.

By the junction with its annular horse trough, public conveniences underground and seats whereon sat the elderly, the trams rattled by on the way to the terminal at Alderman Newton's School Playing Fields and Western Park or into the city centre by way of Applegate Hill.

In the early twenties when our milkman, with pegleg, cycled one-footed from customer to customer with his small churn hanging from the handlebars and bread was delivered daily from a horsedrawn van bearing the name Price, the lamplighter did his evening rounds with a long pole to light the street gas lamps, whilst at the junction a news vendor was shouting some words I never understood but which still ring in my ears as 'jex-jo'. Across the road the library closed about nine o'clock after housing readers and sleepers alike in its reading room where the newspapers were held down by metal strips and journals neatly contained within black folders.

At this time Narborough road was largely residential from the junction to Shaftesbury road, terraced houses were fronted by small gardens and iron gates and railings, later to be removed to help the war effort. A few shops there were on the odd side near to Hinckley Road; Leedham's, cycle shop; a general store run by Mr. and Mrs. Brooks, the recipients of many Saturday pennies and the office of Monk's furniture removals who lived further along the block. Apart from two entries, the only gap amongst the frontages was for Mayser – ironmonger, at number forty-five. The main shopping area began at Shaftesbury road with Mr. Bird's cycle and electrical supplies shop. There, with the advent of radio and football and other sporting commentaries, a knot of people would gather on Saturday afternoon to listen to the broadcast via a large horn loudspeaker over the shop door, just as some people watch television sport through shop windows today. Opposite at the corner of Roman street stood Squires – bakers and confectioners – where sometimes one was lucky enough to see sacks of flour being hoisted to an upper level. Apart from Dr. Green and Dr. Cooper at opposite corners of Westcotes Drive and a hall by Harrow road which was, I understand, a British Restaurant in wartime, shops occupied most of the area on both sides to the schools at Upperton road.

Beyond the schools on the even side was the local cinema, the 'Olympia', its manager, a portly figure commonly known to children as 'Fatty Grey', often stood outside supervising the queues as they gathered, particularly for the children's matinee on Saturday afternoons spent in the company of such stars as Tom Mix, Hoot Gibson and the local pianist. As years passed and tenants passed on or left, houses lost their front gardens to become shops and attendant accommodation. One remembers Mr. Mossman starting a photographic business and a block of four shops opposite to the library opening up at various intervals. These included a milliner, a wholesale tea merchant, and a sweet shop cum tobacconist but most memorable of all was the one next door which was, at various times, a greengrocery, and the headquarters of the local branch of Oswald Mosley's blackshirt party until its windows were smashed by a rival faction.

In contrast to Narborough road, the Hinckley road led through a predominantly shopping area, and became mostly residential from Fosse road to the Western Park. Returning as ever to the junction and one is led naturally into Braunstone Gate, reminding the writer of daily walks to school in the thirties past Hall and Earls's factory and various shops with names still remembered: Tuckwood, Calow, Bloxham and Gadsby with Sturgess' garage opposite at the corner of Bede street. Here at the Boulevard we could proceed via Kirby and West's new factory with a peep at the automatic bottling machine in action and thence through the Castle Gardens when open or along Duns lane past The Wheatsheaf factory and the West Bridge with a glimpse to the left of the long dole queues at the Centre on the hill.

A description of the junction area of the West End would not be complete without mention of Great Holme street, an uninteresting thoroughfare of small terraced houses, corner shops and factories which, to me, seemed never to live up to its high sounding name.

Mrs. Fitzgerald now lives in Kirby Muxloe. Her grandfather, Harry North, opened a butcher's shop at 21, Ridley Street, whilst the present shop was being built nearly 100 years ago. She reports that on the first day only ¼lb of suet was sold!

The working hours were very long and hard, the shop was opened early in the morning – 4.30 a.m. on Friday and Saturday and it was often mid-night before they finished. Meat was delivered by pony and trap. Tommy the pony was kept in Gimsons Field. My Grandmother had to work very hard as well as helping in the shop. When my Grandmother was cooking, there was a black range in the kitchen – the oven was heated by the fire – cakes and puddings were cooked in large meat tins. The range was black, it had to be black-leaded to clean it – it was a special cleaner called Zebra – it looked like black shoe polish – this grate and method of cooking was used for the first few years I lived at the shop with my parents.

Life as I remember it was very quiet years ago with very little traffic on the road – a few cars and no city buses – we had trams for transport, these used to run to the terminus at Western Park. When they came back into town they seemed to travel very fast down Hinckley Road and sway from side to side. We could get a two penny transfer ticket which allowed you to change trams at the Clock Tower and travel as far as London road station. We used to have two ice-cream men that came round on their tricycle's, the Walls man and the Eldorado ice cream man – the Walls man had a dark blue and white ice cream box on his tricycle and wore a dark blue cap and jacket. We had to put a piece of card with a W on it if we wanted one. I remember we could buy penny snow fruits – these were triangle shaped frozen ice about six inches long – various flavours – the ice would be called sorbet today. Every Friday morning the fish man would travel up and down the cobbled streets with his horse drawn cart and the rabbits swinging backwards and forwards on an iron rod above his cart.

We often had the rag and bone man going round the streets shouting 'rag and bones'. They always gave a goldfish in a jam jar in exchange for old clothes. On Fridays the knife grinder always called at the butchers shops to sharpen any knives – he pushed his grinding stone around on a truck – the stone was connected to a footpiece by an iron rod which stone had to be kept wet. My Father did all the cooked meats. Faggots were also made then sent to the bakehouse in large baking trays. They were sold hot with gravy on a Friday night. Customers used to order them by leaving their basins at the shop on Friday morning with a note in as to how many they wanted. They cost two pence each.

We had milk delivered twice a day, a Mrs. Derbyshire came very early in the morning at about 6 a.m. from her shop across the road in Andrews Street carrying her milk churn and measure – then later in the morning Mr. Hobill came with his horse and cart, and measured into a jug how much milk mother wanted – it was lovely, rich and creamy milk.

Clarks – the greengrocer on the opposite corner to us on Ridley Street always sold home made pickled onions and red cabbage. We always had to save our old jam jars for Mrs. Clark. Vinegar was sold out of a wooden barrel – people either took a jug or a bottle for their vinegar. Every night either Mr. or Mrs. Clark would soak some dried peas ready to sell next day to their customers, as no one had thought of freezing vegetables.

Half way up Ridley Street there was an outdoor off licence which belonged to the Northampton Brewery – an elephant was their trade-mark. Beer was sold out of the barrel; the local people used to go with their jugs for a pint of beer to have with their supper.

Years ago a pageant of Leicester was held and all the various shops were set out, my father set a pig with two heads in the centre of the shop with my doll sitting on its back. A clock and the telephone number was made out of sausages and the City of Leicester Coat of Arms in the centre of the front window was made out of coloured suet. My Father won an award for this effort. The Daily Express also ran a similar competition which he won.

Mr. Lenton also submitted his entry on tape. He was born in Wilberforce Road and is a founder member of the Leicester Textile Society. In 1930 he was a part time lecturer at the Leicester Technical School.

Now there were no houses at all on the right hand side of Narborough road after Imperial avenue. They were all fields with the exception of a small group of allotments which went down to what is now Braunstone avenue. There was a footpath there which went to Braunstone. In the corner of the field which adjoined Imperial avenue they used to bring the sheep there to be dipped and there was a farmhouse set obliquely at the end of the field and that farmhouse, I believe, is still there with the new houses that were built in 1919. Now, at the top of Narborough road at the top of the hill there, there was a small area set out as a riding school where they used to bring the horses from a stable somewhere on the right-hand side of Churchgate, for practice with the pupils who were learning how to ride.

I went to Narborough School, and when we were probably about eight

Corner of Applegate Street. (Illustration by Paul Barrand from an original photograph courtesy of the Leicester Mercury.)

years old there were so many children that we were taken across the road to Robert Hall School and stayed there until we were about 11 years old and then came back into the main buildings where we were segregated. Prior to that, of course, it was girls and boys. I stayed there until I was 14 years old. The school was on the main road from Narborough and Enderby where you are from the country. So on sheep days, market days that is – when they were going to bring the cattle or the sheep into the cattle market, there would be droves of sheep coming down the Narborough road and it would be impossible to get by for the sheep spilled right over the road and the pavements. It was a very interesting sight. I remember quite well that at school about 1916, we sat in classes cutting out felt for gas masks for the soldiers – we thought they might need them which they did. They were just felt, white felt. It stuck in my mind for many, many years.

Going right down to Narborough road then, we come to the corner and the building is still there although the front has been altered – the coffee shop. One of the old coffee shops that were typical in the town at Churchgate and down Wharf Street and in those places you could get a cup of tea for a penny or tuppence. Above that was a billiards saloon. The building has been altered to a shop. It's almost on the corner of Braunstone Gate.

Now, coming back to when the Olympia Cinema was built in 1913 and the surprising thing about that was that there must have been a contract to have it built in a certain time for they used to have electric lights on in the night and the chaps worked all through the night to get the building finished. It was really a very good cinema. We used to go as it was quite near to us and the others like Fosse and in other areas on the East side weren't built. So it was quite something for us.

One of the most important things that happened to the West End was when the Adult School was built just along Western road – now a hosiery factory.

The amazing thing is that I've got about thirty newsletters describing the activities of the school, and in its heyday there would be as many as 200 men and 150 women. There was a young men's class and a women's class. There were all sorts of organisations that met during the week. They started in a little building – I'm not quite sure where you could actually find it. They moved into Noble Street – a little factory – and then bought the mortgage for this building. I remember at every annual meeting they'd say, 'Well the mortgage is now reduced to such and such.' But obviously some men, quite a few were really influential men, businessmen with money, put up money for the mortgage.

One became a member of the institute by paying perhaps 5 shillings a year and then you could go in any time and play cards. There was a gas pipe brought down the wall and it was always kept lit so that when men were smoking pipes or cigarettes they could just go and put their pipe to this little gas light and light their pipes.

We would congregate at 9 o'clock and open with a hymn, and there would be a prayer, another hymn and the first Sunday of every month we had what was called an open Sunday and our Secretary would arrange for speakers in the community to come. But the other three Sundays we would break up into classes.

On Mondays it would be the girls' meeting. There would be about 30 or 40 who would have their meeting in a similar way. They would have a talk and perhaps a discussion. Tuesday evening would be the ladies' evening – the mothers – and they were 150 strong. Wednesdays it would be perhaps used for some other thing. Thursdays, in the summertime, someone might arrange for a mid-week dance or a little social. Thursdays, in the winter, the girls had a gymnasium class run by a lady teacher because they would be in their tunics. And at 9 o'clock, for quite a while we used to press and press the committee to allow us to go up at 9 o'clock to learn dancing, what we might call now Old Time Dancing. I can see myself now going up the stairs there, a dozen boys or so, young fellows like me 16 or perhaps 17 waiting at the door so we could go in and learn how to dance. Of course we learned how to do the waltz and the twostep and the barn dance and dances like that.

Saturday night we had socials or dances. There was a tennis club, a gymnasium, a hockey club and they would all arrange in turn to have a dance or alternatively there would be a social evening. In the centre of the floor there would be rows of chairs set and we'd go along and pay 6d and sit there and listen to someone sing or tell a story and then have a dance and refreshments and then come home at 10 o'clock after having a wonderful night.

Mrs. Smith now lives in Nottingham but was born in Pool Road. Like Mr. Williams she also writes about the Newfoundpool area and says she is 'proud to be a West-Ender'.

First on the left as you climbed the hill was Hodges greengrocery and general store. Hodges had a fine selection of sweets and was the first shop on the Pool to sell homemade ice lollies at one penny each. Next to Hodges was Oaks Dairy where you could buy milk from the churn. Ice-cream was sold by the scoop and dispensed into your own basin. The pleasure of visiting the dairy with its sweet, milky smell and gleaming apparatus was somewhat diminished by the thought of the race home up the hill to save the ice-cream from melting. Perhaps this is why I still prefer mine a little on the soft side.

Shooters shop was half-way up the hill. It was much smaller than Hodges, being an ordinary house with the front room and window converted for business. We were forbidden to spend our precious pennies at Shooters as Mam had had a difference of opinion with the proprietor over the quality of some purchase. Occasionally we were tempted in by the display of apples and oranges and sought to conceal our purchase till we were well away from the shop. 'I'll tell your Mam you've been in Shooters!' was a dire threat from any of our playmates. If carried out, it resulted in next week's pennies being withheld.

Blands shop was at the top of the hill on the corner of Rowan Street. It was a fascinating place, ill-lit in winter, but well-stocked. Sugar was weighed out into blue bags. There was a bell on the heavy wooden door that jangled merrily to call the owner from the dark cavern of the living rooms behind the shop. When Mary Price took over, we shopped there often. She was a friend of my Aunt and would often slip us a sweet or stick of black licquorice. Fred Freeman kept the off-licence at the corner of Ruby Street. He was a big florid man and had pumps behind the counter where he pulled foaming beer into jugs for his customers. The bakehouse was almost opposite Prices. At

Christmas, Mam sometimes mixed the cake and took it to the bakehouse to be cooked along with others in the big ovens. In Hawthorne Street was Smith's Coalyard. The business was run by two thin and silent brothers. It was Mr. Jack Smith with whom we had dealings. He provided a large part of our income. As well as being a coal merchant, he was also a scrap dealer. We collected jam jars and old clothes, especially woollens, and took our booty round to the yard. We watched him anxiously as he examined our offerings. All chipped or cracked jars were rejected. Our rags were sorted and weighed. Then he would look at us, unsmiling and businesslike, and offer a price. We nodded vigorously whatever he said, and he counted the coins into our palm. Sometimes it was great wealth, and took all of us to the Fosse pictures.

Although we made occasional trips to the parks – Fosse, Abbey and Western – Pool Road was our playground. There was little traffic. Cyclists rang their bells for us to clear a way. We felt the whole area belonged to us. In Summer Mam opened the front door of the house and our dolls and toys spilled over the step and across the pavement. As we grew, so did our play area, and we wandered the Pool with kites made from newspaper, hoops and sticks and whip and top. Buttons was another of our games. Our own collection was spread along the pavement. Our opponent crouched behind a chalked line and flicked his buttons towards ours. He claimed any he touched. This could also be played with 'fag cards' and fag cards could be made up into complete sets that were highly prized. Games of skill – like snobs and double-ball, filled up many hours. If they were played competitively it was for the honour of winning and carried no prize.

We had two street parties on the Pool to mark the end of the war. One was for V.E. (Victory in Europe) Day and one for the final victory in 1945. Benches and tables were borrowed from the schools and erected at the top of Pool Road hill. Old sheets, trimmed with red, white and blue paper, served as tablecloths. A great feast was made, such as we had not seen during the lean, austere years between 1939-45. We had sandwiches of meat and fish, iced cakes and great jellies made from fruity crystals and jugs of homemade lemonade. We searched our small store of clothes for patriotic colours and wore ribbons in our hair. We spent weeks crayoning banners to welcome home our heroes, and made bunting to hang across the streets. There was dancing after tea and the merry-making went on long after we had fallen asleep and been carried off to our beds. The community spirit that marked those days was part of my childhood. The Pool was a good place to live – a good place to grow up.

Mr. Warren's entry was submitted on tape. He was born in Foxon Street in 1914 and served as an Air Raid Warden during the Second World War. He was one of the first 'talking pictures' projectionists in the country and founded the Leicester City Darts League, of which he was General Secretary for 41 years.

First we'll take Braunstone Gate where the Co-operative Stables used to be, just inside Bede Street where every morning prompt at 8.15 you'd see 40 dray horses come out of their stables in single file and walk round to the bridge yard which was on the Boulevard. This is now the BRS depot. It was a

The Olympia Cinema on the Narborough Road and Walton Street corner. (Illustration by Paul Barrand from an original photograph courtesy of Leicestershire Museums, Art Galleries and Records Service.)

wonderful sight to see, always fascinating. And just above on the other side where the Castle Gardens now stand, there used to be allotments owned by an old man who spent most of his time going round the streets with a truck and a spade getting the horse manure for the allotments. Also he used to sell a lot to the gardeners. There were mountains of it. And where Castle Gardens now stand, after his death in about 1938, I think the Corporation took it over then and made a beautiful little park of it – really beautiful. A bit lower down, just on the Boulevard opposite New Park street stood a small picture house. Only a small building but it was used as a picture house then for many years. And then when the pictures finally closed it was taken over for the use of boxing where Larry Gains, Reggie Nene and Phil Scott all fought big fights. These all were later taken over by the Granby Halls, and afterwards this was turned into a skating rink which lasted for about two years and now that is an educational department.

Then we go a little further round to Duns Lane. At the bottom of the railway bridge there used to be a little pub there called the Old Talbot and that had many strange things happen inside. For instance, on a Sunday dinnertime, once a month, a fellow used to go in there, a smartly dressed fellow with a sack on his back and the moment he entered the pub all the customers in the bar would stand on their seats and then the man would take his coat off and put his false teeth on the bar and put his hand in the sack and fetch out three big rats which he let free in the bar. He would afterwards stalk them on his hands and knees and worry them with his gums. This was all done for charity. He used to go around the bar and smokeroom and collect nearly as much as £5 on just one Sunday dinnertime. Very few people realised in those days that this man was doing it for charity. Then we can pop over the road on to King Richard's road next to the West Bridge wharf. In those days there was very little motorisation. Everything was done by horse and cart. But what you could do there was to go and borrow a truck from the wharf and put 2 cwt. of coal which was 1s. 1d. a cwt. and take it home and then return the truck. I had a barrow myself to fetch this coal for different neighbours and I earned myself many a penny on a Saturday morning.

Then we can come back to Braunstone Gate where Casey's Pawn Shop stood at the corner of New Park street, run by a man named Mr. Eames. On a Monday morning you'd see queues outside waiting to pawn some of their clothes for just a few shillings to last a week. A man's average wage in those days was only between £2 and 50s. And you could also see the same crowd on a Friday waiting to redeem their goods. There was also Calow's the Barbers on Braunstone Gate which still stands. Mr. Calow himself used to cut my father's hair and he even cut mine on my wedding day which was 50 years ago. Then there was Tuckwood's the little cake shop with lovely vanilla slices in the shop window at 1d each. I used to fetch the fresh cakes from their other bakery which stood on the corner of Upperton road. For this I got a bag of stale cakes which my mother greatly appreciated, I assure you. And then going on to the Western road which was always a hive of industry: Equity Shoes, Magic Polish Company, Potter's, all of them existed in those days. It has changed very little since then. And then on the corner of Briton street stood Wand's Chemists – a beautiful chemist shop with a great big shop floor. I used to work there when I was twelve, part-time. I'd go in at 4.30-6.30 every day and Saturdays all day, for which I received the sum of 4s. And afterwards on a Saturday when the shop was shut I had to scrub the shop floor.

Going into Westcotes Drive, at the bottom there have always been the surgeries of various doctors. In the 1930s and before even, Dr. Greer and Dr. Cooper had their surgery at number two. This surgery had been made from old stables and is still in existence today. Further up the Westcotes Drive, there was Westcotes Maternity Home, a lovely little building with beautiful gardens in front. At the top of Westcotes Drive there used to be a farm and it was all fields there where we used to go scrumping on a Sunday afternoon. In those days if you went to the doctor privately, in the private home, you used to have to get all your prescriptions from the chemist, but if you went to a National Health doctor you received a prescription which you had to take to a medical dispensary which stood on the corner of Tyndale Street and Hinckley Road. Here you queued for your prescriptions and if you needed a bottle you'd be charged a penny on the bottle.

There was very little electricity in the West End at that time from 1928-1936. All the streets had gas lamps and as regards electricity, very few people had it because in those days it was quite expensive. When I was 16 I was an apprentice electrician in the West End of Leicester and I think I electrified no less than 400 homes. I was also greatly interested in the cinema. I loved pictures and every Saturday afternoon we used to go to the 'Tudor', pay 1d to go in and when you got inside the manager used to stand there with a parrot on his shoulder and give everybody three toffees or a chewing gum.

I was so fascinated with the pictures, I was determined that when I could leave school at the age of 14 I would like to get in as a projectionist and this I did. I went to the Floral Hall when I was 14½ as assistant projectionist and used to have to stand there turning the handles from 2 o'clock in the afternoon till 10 o'clock at night as in those days they had no electric motors there. But then in June 1929 the Palace next door which had been showing musicals for a number of years decided to have the first talking pictures in Great Britain. I put in for a job as assistant projectionist at the Palace and succeeded. There we opened on the 29th of June 1929 with Al Jolson in 'The Singing Fool'. I was really proud of that. And I'm pleased to say that although I miss all the picture houses in Leicester, I have great memories. I finished my projection days at the Olympia Picture House which stood on the corner of Walton street and Stuart street and top prices were 1s. for the balcony and 9d. for the stalls. You couldn't get over the doorstep now for that price.